3 1994 01072 0271

D0467667

Birds up close

Marine Birds

J 598.177 KAL
Kalman, Bobbie
Marine birds

FEB 2 4 2001

$19.96
CENTRAL   31994010720271

A Bobbie Kalman Book
Crabtree Publishing Company

Birds up close

A Bobbie Kalman Book

**For Christopher,
who is happiest at sea**

Editor-in-Chief
Bobbie Kalman

Writing team
Bobbie Kalman
Jacqueline Langille
Niki Walker

Text research
Jacqueline Langille
Tara Harte
April Fast

Managing editor
Lynda Hale

Series editor
Niki Walker

Editor
Greg Nickles

Photo research
Jacqueline Langille

Computer design
Lynda Hale
Andy Gecse (cover concept)

Consultant
Louis Bevier, Academy of Natural Sciences, Philadelphia, PA

Production coordinator
Hannelore Sotzek

Photographs
Jim Bryant: page 20
James Kamstra: pages 11 (top), 18 (bottom right), 26
Diane Payton Majumdar: pages 12 (top), 14, 15 (top)
Robert McCaw: pages 11 (bottom), 13, 15 (bottom), 18 (left), 28-29
Tom Stack & Associates: Gerald & Buff Corsi: page 10; Rod Planck: page 6;
  Milton Rand: page 4
Sylvia Stevens: cover, pages 7, 12 (bottom), 16, 21, 24, 25 (both)
Dave Taylor: pages 5 (left), 23, 28 (left)
Valan Photos: Fred Bruemmer: page 27; John Cancalosi: page 30;
  John Eastcott & Yva Momatiuk: back cover; J.R. Page: page 9
Jerry Whitaker: title page, pages 8, 17

Illustration
Barbara Bedell: page 19

Printer
Worzalla Publishing Company

Color separations and film
Dot 'n Line Image Inc.
CCS Princeton (cover)

Crabtree Publishing Company

350 Fifth Avenue
Suite 3308
New York
N.Y. 10118

360 York Road, RR 4,
Niagara-on-the-Lake,
Ontario, Canada
L0S 1J0

73 Lime Walk
Headington
Oxford OX3 7AD
United Kingdom

Copyright © **1998 CRABTREE PUBLISHING COMPANY**.
All rights reserved. No part of this publication may be
reproduced, stored in a retrieval system or be transmitted
in any form or by any means, electronic, mechanical,
photocopying, recording, or otherwise, without the prior
written permission of Crabtree Publishing Company.

Cataloging in Publication Data
Kalman, Bobbie
  Marine birds

(Birds up close)
Includes index.

ISBN 0-86505-752-4 (library bound)   ISBN 0-86505-766-4 (pbk.)
This book introduces the eating habits, breeding, nesting, and
survival techniques of birds that live on, in, or near salt water.

1. Sea birds—Juvenile literature. [1. Sea birds. 2. Birds.]
I. Title. II. Series: Kalman, Bobbie. Birds up close.

QL676.2.K348 1997   j598.177   LC 97-39875
                                              CIP

Contents

Living on the ocean

Marine birds are birds that live on the ocean or along ocean coastlines. They find all their food in the salt water of oceans and seas. Most marine birds are **pelagic**, which means they spend most of their time swimming in or flying over open water. They return to shore only to breed and raise their young.

From puffins to boobies

There are more than 350 types of marine birds. To make these birds easier to study, scientists group the ones with similar appearances and habits into **families**. There are several families of marine birds, including the gull, gannet, auk, and penguin families.

(below) Tufted puffins live on the Pacific Ocean. They belong to the auk family.

(opposite, left) Many shore birds live on marine coasts only at certain times of the year. They rely on finding food in areas where a beach meets the ocean.

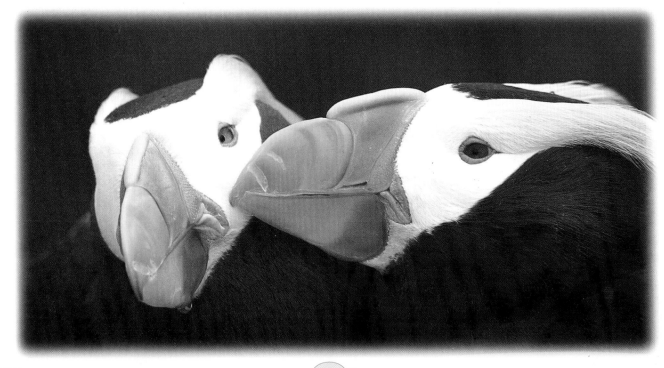

Swimmers or fliers

Most marine birds are excellent fliers, and many also swim well. Some birds such as albatrosses and petrels spend most of their life flying. Auks prefer to swim. They make only short flights. Penguins, on the other hand, use their wings just for swimming.

Doing everything together

Many marine birds are **social**, which means they hunt, nest, and travel in a group. They hunt together when they find a large **school**, or group, of fish near the surface of the water. Most marine birds nest in large groups at nesting sites called **colonies**. When some **migrate**, or travel, to warmer areas in the winter, they usually fly in groups.

willet

Cape gannet

(above) Gannets are marine birds that are found all over the world. The Northern gannet lives in the north, and the Cape gannet lives in the south.

Water bodies

Marine birds have bodies that are built for living on or near water. They have special legs, feet, and bills. The birds stay warm when they swim or dive because their feathers keep the water from reaching their skin.

A stretchy mouth helps a marine bird swallow prey whole.

Waterproof covering

Feathers provide natural waterproofing. They lock together and cover a bird's body like a raincoat. Birds **preen**, or comb, their feathers to keep them in place. Oil from a **preen gland** near the base of their tail keeps their feathers smooth. Some scientists think the preening oil makes the feathers more waterproof. Many marine birds have a larger preen gland than other types of birds.

Long, strong legs are useful for swimming.

Webbed feet act as paddles.

Webbed feet and strong legs

Most birds have thin legs and toes for perching on branches. Marine birds, on the other hand, have strong legs and webbed feet (shown left) for swimming. The skin between their toes makes their feet like paddles. Their paddle-like feet push against the water and help the birds swim.

Fishing bills

All birds have a beak that is suited to the type of food they eat. Marine birds have a long, strong bill for catching and holding onto slippery fish. Some, such as cormorants, have a hook on their upper bill for grabbing fish. Gulls use their sharp bill to rip and tear their prey. Like all birds, marine birds have a protective covering on their beak. Parts of this covering wear out and fall off, especially along the edges. To replace worn parts, the covering always grows, just as people's fingernails do.

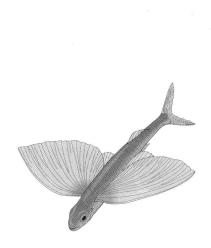

Tubenoses

Most birds have their nostrils inside their bill. The nostril hole opens on the surface of the bill near their head. Albatrosses, shearwaters, storm petrels, fulmars, and diving petrels belong to a family of marine birds called **tubenoses**.

Tubenoses have their nostrils on the outside of their bill, as shown on this giant petrel. Short nostril tubes sit on top of the bill. The nostril tubes open on each side of the upper bill (see page 10), or they are joined on top, as shown right.

Marine meals

Fish is an important part of a marine bird's diet. More than half of all marine birds eat mainly fish. They catch only fish that they can swallow whole. Smaller marine birds eat small fish such as anchovies. Big birds such as cormorants eat larger types of fish, including cod and haddock. A few types of marine birds eat large amounts of **krill**, a tiny sea animal that is similar to shrimp.

Runny noses

Most birds and animals can drink only fresh water. Marine birds, however, drink salt water every day. There is also a lot of salt on the fish they eat. Too much salt is unhealthy for any animal, so marine birds have a special way of getting rid of the salt they eat. They have **salt glands** near their eyes. These glands take the extra salt out of a marine bird's body. They make a salty fluid that leaks out of the bird's nostrils and runs down its beak. The dripping liquid causes the bird to have a constantly runny nose.

Junk food

Unlike most marine birds, herring gulls no longer
need to live near the ocean to find food. They once
ate mainly fish and shellfish, but now they eat
almost anything. They feed on the scraps thrown off
fishing boats and the garbage dumped at landfill
sites. In towns and cities that are near lakes and
rivers, gulls eat food dropped on the ground or in
trash bins. They feast on everything from hot dogs
to potato chips. Although this food is not part of
their natural diet, more gulls move inland to feed
on it every year. Many gulls now live far from their
usual ocean home.

*People pollute the oceans with
garbage that washes up on shore.
Gulls and other marine birds
mistake small white objects for
food. The gull above has a piece
of cardboard. When a bird eats
this type of garbage, its stomach
becomes blocked, causing the
bird to die.*

Breeding and nesting

Most marine birds return to the same breeding site each year. They find their partner, breed, and then raise their chicks. Breeding sites are usually at the edge of the sea, where birds nest on cliffs or in burrows dug into the ground. Many marine birds breed with the same **mate**, or partner, each year.

Albatrosses cannot breed every year because they need a long time to raise their baby. For some types of albatrosses, more than a year passes between the time the egg is laid and the time the chick leaves the nest.

Courting a mate

To win a mate, most birds do a special dance called a **courtship display**. Even though marine birds have the same mate from year to year, they still do a courtship display when they meet one another at the breeding site. They dance to show that they recognize each other and still want to be partners.

Building a nest

After they breed, most marine birds make a nest for their eggs. Some pile grass, plants, and seaweed on a cliff ledge. Others build a large mound of mud and grass or a nest of sticks in a tree. A few marine birds such as boobies lay their eggs on the ground.

(above) During their courtship display, boobies point their beaks toward the sky.

(below) Seaweed makes a great nest.

Raising young

When the eggs of most marine birds hatch, the babies, or **chicks**, need a lot of care. They need their parents to feed them and protect them from **predators**. A predator is an animal that hunts other animals for food. Only a few types of marine birds take their young chicks to sea with them. Most chicks wait in their nest for their parents to return with food. Some parents take turns guarding the nest.

(top) Newly hatched marine bird chicks are weak and helpless.

(above) Chicks need to be fed many times a day.

Bringing home fish

Fish-eating birds have several ways of bringing food back to their young. Some carry one or two small fish at a time in their beak. They have to make several hunting trips each day. Others swallow their prey before returning to their nest. At the nest, they bring up the food for their chicks to eat. A few types of marine birds store food in special cheek pouches until they have enough to bring back to their chick.

Protecting their young

The thousands of birds nesting in a colony offer chicks good protection from predators. If an enemy comes too close, many birds attack it. They swoop at the enemy's head, biting and scratching to drive it away.

Marine birds sit on their chicks to keep them warm. The gannet on the right puts its chick on top of its webbed feet.

They're everywhere!

Gulls are found in almost every part of the world. Some types of gulls have even moved inland away from salt water. They like the food they find at landfill sites. Today, some "sea" gulls never see the ocean in their lifetime! Unlike most birds, gulls can get around in almost any landscape because they walk, swim, and fly with ease. Other birds can usually do only one of these things well.

Older gulls are the leaders of the flocks. Young gulls must keep their neck pulled close to their body. If not, their lifted head is an invitation to fight. The older gull usually wins these fights.

Bottomless stomach

Gulls eat huge amounts of food. They seem to be hungry all the time! They can eat larger prey than most birds. Their wide mouth and stretchy throat allow them to swallow whole eggs, large fish, young birds, small rodents, and even steak bones.

More about gulls

Types: 45 species

Length: Up to 30 inches (76 cm)

Weight: 2 - 4$\frac{1}{2}$ pounds (1 - 2 kg)

Life span: Up to 25 years

Food: Fish, meat, vegetables, insects, plants, garbage, and other birds' eggs and chicks

Predators: Foxes, hedgehogs, weasels, skunks, rats, and humans

Related birds: Skuas, terns, noddies, skimmers, auks, and phalaropes

Cranky comrades

Gulls feed in groups and nest in large colonies. They like to be around one another, but they often fight. Sometimes they fight over food, but often they fight each other simply because one gull comes too close to another. In a colony, adult gulls peck neighboring chicks that come too close to their nest. They sometimes peck so hard that they kill a chick. To show who's boss, older gulls bite young gulls, as shown in the picture above.

(right) Birds need to stretch their muscles in the same way people do. This gull is stretching its wings to keep them ready for flying.

15

What a mouthful!

Most people can recognize a puffin. Its penguin-like markings and striped beak make it easy to identify. Each year during breeding season, the puffin's beak becomes even brighter. Colorful plates grow over the beak as part of the bird's courtship display. These plates fall off at the end of the summer.

How many can they carry?

Puffins can carry many fish in their beak at once, as shown on the opposite page. Some can hold up to 60 small fish called sand eels. They usually bring back between four and 20 fish to feed their chick at the nest.

(opposite) Puffins carry fish onto land only when they have a chick to feed.

(below) Puffins have small wings. These birds do not fly as well as gulls or dive as well as penguins. Their wings are more suited to swimming underwater.

More about puffins

Types: 4 species

Height: 7 - 12 inches (18 - 30 cm)

Weight: 14 - 30 ounces (400 - 840 g)

Life span: 25 years

Food: Sand eels, herring, haddock, and other small fish

Predators: rats, Arctic foxes, skuas, gulls, falcons, and humans

Related birds: Other auks; also gulls, terns, skimmers, and phalaropes

Sky-pointers

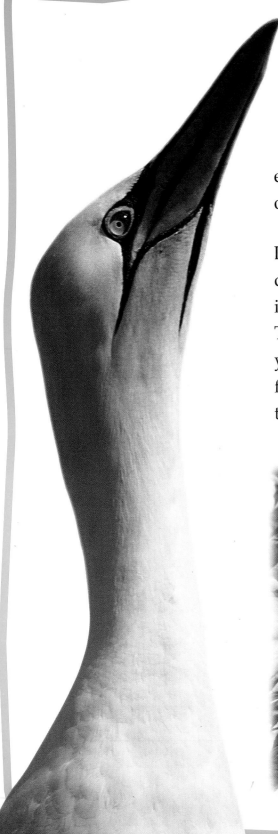

Gannets are strong fliers that often dive for their food. They also steal food from other seabirds. They are **scavengers**, which means they sometimes eat dead fish or garbage that they find in the water or on the shore.

During the breeding season, gannets perform a courtship display called **sky-pointing**. A bird points its bill in the air as a signal that it recognizes its mate. This signal helps a pair of birds bond from year to year. When one bird returns to the nest after hunting for food, partners greet each other by stretching out their wings and banging their bills together.

Plunge divers

Gannets usually **plunge dive** to catch their food. Birds plunge dive when they drop straight down into the water from high in the air, as shown below. When a gannet spots a school of fish, it flies to a great height. It keeps its eyes on the fish far below and then dives straight down, dropping like a rock. The bird plunges headfirst into the waves at high speed and catches a fish underwater. Air pockets in the gannet's skull absorb the shock of hitting the water and prevent damage to the bird's brain. The gannet swims to the surface to swallow its prey.

More about gannets

Types: 3 species
Length: 3 feet (90 cm)
Weight: 5 - 8 pounds (2 - 3.6 kg)
Life span: 20 years
Food: Fish
Related birds: Tropic birds, pelicans, boobies, cormorants, anhingas, and frigate birds

Big, bright feet

Boobies are large, colorful birds that are related to gannets. The birds' brightly colored feet and bills and bare face patches have earned them the nickname "clowns." People named them "boobies" because they thought the birds were stupid for allowing humans near them. In the past, people killed millions of boobies for food because they were so easy to catch.

Boobies lay their eggs on the ground. To keep the eggs warm, the birds gently cover the eggs with their feet. All species of boobies warm their egg with their webbed feet.

See my great feet!

Male boobies fly over their nesting site to show others they own that area. When they land, they hold their feet in front of their body to attract their mate. The male blue-footed booby also marches around his female partner as part of his courtship display. He lifts his feet high off the ground to show off their bright color to his mate.

Taking the plunge

Boobies plunge dive for their food in the same way gannets do. Boobies fly over the ocean looking for large schools of fish. When some types spot fish, they whistle to call other boobies to the area. A group gathers, and the birds dive into the water at the same time. They can dive from great heights and often hit the water at high speed.

Built for diving

When boobies plunge dive from high in the air, they hit the water very hard. Most birds break their bones when they crash into things, but boobies have special body parts to protect them. In their throat and chest, they have small pouches filled with air that absorb the shock of hitting the water.

Unlike most other types of boobies, which nest on the ground, red-footed boobies build their nests in low trees.

More about boobies

Types: 6 species
Length: 2 - 3 feet (61 - 90 cm)
Weight: 2 - 8 pounds (1 - 3.6 kg)
Life span: 20 years
Food: Fish
Related birds: Tropic birds, gannets, cormorants, anhingas, frigate birds, and pelicans

Only the brown ones

Most pelicans live mainly on freshwater lakes and rivers. Brown pelicans are the only type that lives on or near salt water. Pelicans are large birds that are awkward on land, but they are skilled fliers.

Dive and scoop

Most pelicans swim on the surface of the water and catch fish in their beak. Brown pelicans, however, rely on their flying skills to catch food. They fly low over the water to look for fish near the surface. When they see a fish, they quickly turn themselves in the air and dive almost straight into the water.

Pelicans are large birds, but they are not heavy. They are lightweight for their body size, which helps them fly gracefully through the air.

Fish pouches

A pelican's bill is long, flat, and straight, with a hook at the end. A large fold of skin called a **pouch** hangs from the bottom half of the bill. Pelicans do not store food in their pouch—they use the pouch for fishing.

A pelican uses its pouch to scoop up fish, and then it snaps its bill shut to trap the fish inside. Along with the fish, the bird scoops up a lot of water. The pelican squeezes its pouch skin to push out all the water, and then it swallows the fish whole.

?More about pelicans

Types: 1 marine species;
   6 species live near fresh water
Length: 4 feet (1.2 m)
Weight: 5½ pounds (2.5 kg)
Life span: Up to 25 years
Related birds: Tropic birds, gannets, boobies, cormorants, anhingas, and frigate birds

Pelicans can scoop up to two gallons (7.6 liters) of water in their pouch. They cannot fly until the water drains out.

The wanderers

Albatrosses are the most pelagic of all marine birds. They spend months flying great distances over the oceans. They also have the longest wingspan of marine birds. Great albatrosses, which include wandering and royal albatrosses, can stretch out their wings almost 12 feet (3.7 m) from tip to tip. All albatrosses sleep on the ocean surface and drink salty sea water. They feed on small marine animals and garbage from ships.

More about albatrosses

Types: 14 species
Length: 2 - 4½ feet (71 - 135 cm)
Weight: 9 - 27 pounds (4 - 12 kg)
Wingspan: 6 - 12 feet (1.8 - 3.7 m)
Life span: 30 - 80 years
Food: Squid and jellyfish; also lampreys, flying fish, rockfish, krill, and crabs
Related birds: Fulmars, petrels, and shearwaters

Masters of the air

Violent storms often keep many types of birds from flying, but the wind rarely blows hard enough to keep albatrosses out of the air. Strong winds help these birds fly because their long, narrow wings are perfect for fast gliding. They can fly for hours without ever flapping their wings.

Stuck on the ground

Albatrosses need wind to lift them into the air. Calm weather can leave them stranded on the water or on dry land. Their wings are so long that they hit the ground or water when the birds flap them for takeoff.

(above) Albatross chicks depend on their parents for food.

(below) This albatross pair renews its mating bond with gentle nuzzles.

Expert divers

Penguins spend more than half their lives in the oceans south of the equator. They enjoy swimming in ocean currents that are always cool or cold. Penguins swim very quickly and gracefully, using their wings, or **flippers**, as paddles. They steer with their feet and tail. All species of penguins swim and dive well to find their food underwater. Some penguins can dive as deep as 870 feet (265 m)!

Penguins live on the open sea and along the coasts of Antarctica, South America, South Africa, Australia, New Zealand, and islands in the southern oceans.

Types: 17 species

Length: 1 - 3½ feet (30 - 100 cm)

Weight: 2 - 65 pounds (1 - 29 kg)

Life span: 15 - 20 years

Food: Fish, squid, krill, and crustaceans

Predators: Leopard seals, sea lions, fur seals, orcas, and sharks; skuas and gulls eat penguin eggs and chicks

Related birds: None

Baby penguins

Most female penguins have one or two chicks each year. Both parent penguins look after their chick, keeping it warm and bringing it food. They take turns leaving the nest to hunt. They carry back food in their **crop**, or throat pouch, and bring it up to feed their chick.

A penguin chick grows quickly and, soon, it is as large as its parents. Penguin parents take care of their chick until it finishes growing its adult feathers, which takes about 40 days. Adult feathers and a thick layer of fat under its skin keep a penguin warm in cold waters.

27

Along the shore

Shore birds spend most of their life on beaches and other coastal areas near oceans. These birds are often called **waders** because they wade, or walk, in shallow water to find food. Unlike other marine birds, their toes are not webbed.

Flock flying

To avoid crashing into each other, most birds do not fly very close together, even in flocks. Large flocks of shore birds, however, fly so close together that their wings often touch, as shown right. When an enemy comes too close to a flock on the beach, thousands of shore birds fly up into the sky together. They dart over the water and fly back and forth as though following one bird. They never crash into each other.

(above) Phalaropes are shore birds that spin around in circles and dart about on the water to stir up their prey and bring it to the surface. They eat tiny marine animals, insect larvae, and gnats.

More about shore birds

Types: 9 families that visit sea coasts, including plovers, sandpipers, and oystercatchers

Length: 5 - 27 inches (13 - 69 cm)

Weight: 1 ounce - 2 pounds (28 - 907 g)

Food: Worms, insects, crustaceans, mollusks, and some plants

Predators: Foxes and weasels

Threats: On beaches, humans destroy nesting sites, eggs, and chicks

Ruining their habitat

People are destroying the oceans and threatening the survival of marine birds. People pollute the water with oil, chemicals, and plastic garbage. Some marine birds are now **endangered**, which means they are in danger of disappearing forever.

Plastic trash

Marine birds often mistake trash for food. They are attracted to small, floating objects, which they sometimes swallow. A bird's body cannot break down plastic and rubber bands, so a bird is sometimes killed when it eats this garbage.

The plastic rings from six-packs of cans easily wrap around a bird's neck. The bird cannot breathe or swallow food properly, so it slowly chokes to death. Before you throw out this trash, clip open the rings!

Oil spills

Oil spills kill thousands of marine birds. The oil destroys the waterproofing on their feathers. Without waterproofing, their skin gets wet, and the birds become cold. They also find it more difficult to float on the water. The birds swallow the oil when they try to clean it off their feathers. The oil poisons the birds, and they die.

Over-fishing

Most marine birds eat only fish and other small ocean animals. People sometimes catch too many fish in an area, and the birds are left with nothing to eat. Fishing nets also can be dangerous to marine birds. Puffins and other seabirds that dive for their food often get caught in large fishing nets called **drift nets**.

Words to know

breed To make babies

colony A group of the same type of animals living together

courtship display A set of actions performed to attract a mate

crop A pouch in a bird's throat that stores and grinds food before it moves into the stomach

family A group of animals with similar appearances and habits

marine Describing something related to the sea

mate A partner that an animal needs in order to produce babies

migrate To travel a long distance to find food, water, or a place to raise babies

pelagic Describing things that live in or on the open ocean

plunge dive A quick dive straight down into the water from high above its surface

pouch A baglike part of the body

scavenger A bird that eats dead fish and animals

Index

1 2 3 4 5 6 7 8 9 0   Printed in the U.S.A.   6 5 4 3 2 1 0 9 8 7